An Ose Mountain Thinker.... At His *Work*

+!+!*+*808*+*!+!+

Ahhh…. Yes!

Auctorem House
276 5th Ave, Ste 704-2591
New York, NY 10001
www.auctoremhouse.com
Phone: 1 888-332-7718

Published by Auctorem House: 11/26/2025

ISBN: 978-1-968059-20-0(sc)
ISBN: 978-1-968059-21-7(e)

Library of Congress Control Number: 2025925674

AUCTOREM
HOUSE

SURVIVAL…. Alaska-Style

... sometimes.....
Feels like better
to stay in Bush all
the time

SURVIVAL---- Skills

AND *Magic*

That tent.... Looks kinda strange.... To me....

Ya know what?? That's the way a walltent looks with her ropes let out.... To let snow slide down.... As opposed to building up on tent roof.... SURVIVAL Lesson--- Always let your tent ropes out when being away from Camp in Winter.... Wish I had a photo of collapsed tent.... 2 Springs ago now.... When heavy accumulation of the long Winter's snowfall.... Broke my tent's ridgepole.... Collapsed my tent camp....

Mtn-Man LOL.... But it wasn't one bit funny when I discovered it.... After hiking for half a day to get back in there.... And then.... Find a disaster waiting for me

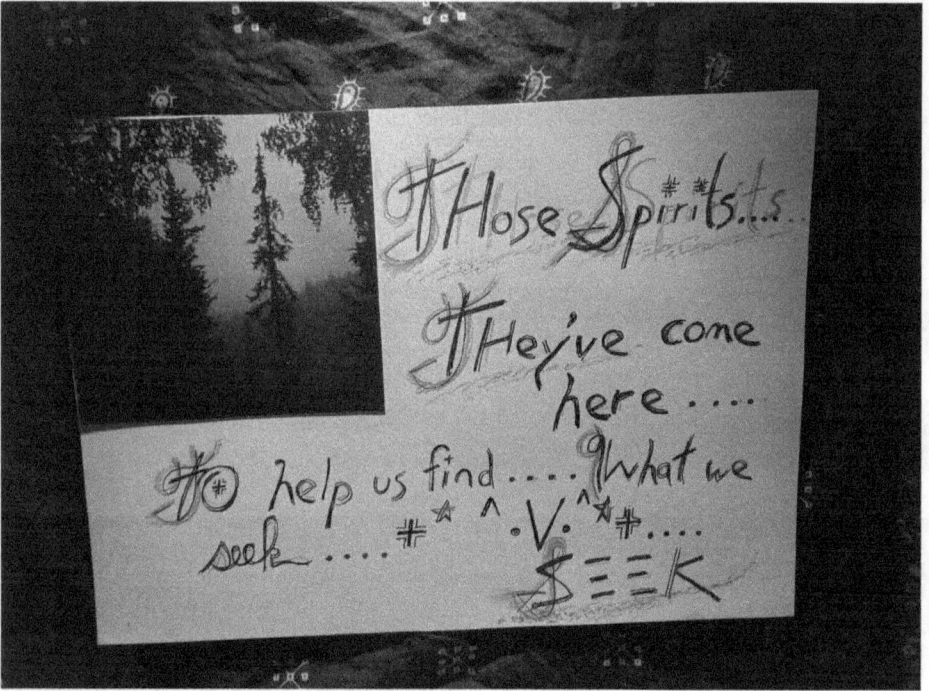

HIGHPOWER CREEK
PUBLISHING

Highpower
Creek
Publishing

.... +*+x ^·V·^ x+*+ ....

A Special Miikwec and THank You…. Going out to Cree Artist Cynthia Saganash, Cree Nation of Waswanipi, QC Canada …. For sharing her stunning Artwork….

Ose Mountain Memoires – Book 2

SURVIVAL

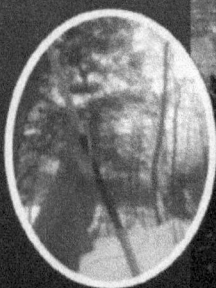

Alaska-Style

Here with us…. On our Front Cover

And THanks to Graphic Artist Melanie Dunhill, UK for our cover's graphics

And now a word about publishing our handmade books—

"HeART-MAde"

… comes another dreamy dreamy rainy rainy afternoon

Been marveling…. MARveling…. At THe TRue Wonders of THings which ARt
      hand-made….
        As are words
            hand-written….

And yes….. We are hand-binding and hand-signing…. AND handing out free copies to our local school and public libraries….

Hey now--- How 'bout….
        "HeART-Made"?

YeA--- "HeART-MAde"….
        THere's a mARvelous Depth
        of Meanings here

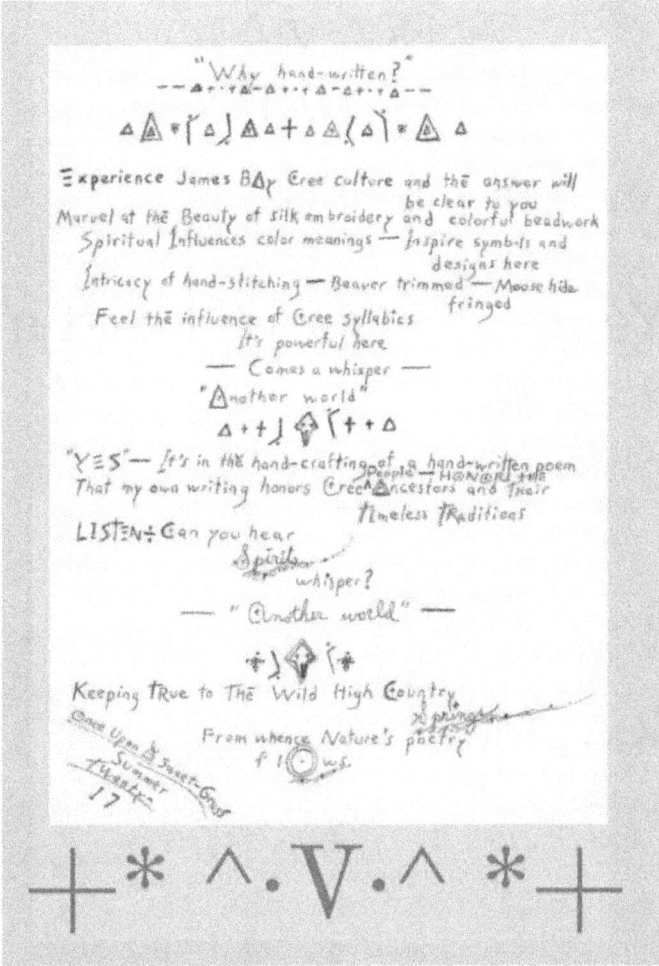

"Why hand-written?"
— — ∆·⊦·⊤∆−∆·⊤ ∆−∆⊤·⊤ ∆ — —

∆ ⬛ ⊦ ⸢∆⸥ ∆ ∆ ⊦ ∆ ⬛ ⸨∆⸩ ⊦ ⬛ ∆

Experience James Bay Cree culture and the answer will
be clear to you
Marvel at the Beauty of silk embroidery and colorful beadwork
Spiritual Influences color meanings — Inspire symbols and
designs here
Intricacy of hand-stitching — Beaver trimmed — Moose hide
fringed
Feel the influence of Cree syllabics
It's powerful here
— Comes a whisper —
"Another world"

∆ ⊦ ⊦ ⸩ ◈ ⸢ ⊦ ⊦ ∆

"YES" — It's in the hand-crafting of a hand-written poem
That my own writing honors Cree Ancestors and their
People — HONOR the
Timeless Traditions

LISTEN÷ Can you hear
Spirit
whisper?

— " Another world " —

⊦ ⸩ ◈ ⸢ ⊦

Keeping True to The Wild High Country
Once Upon A Sweet-Grass   From whence Nature's poetry
Summer   f l Ows.   Springs
Thank-u
17

╋ ✳ ∧ · V · ∧ ✳ ╋

Ahh and Ah-Hey!
HeART-MAde in THe
Workshop
Of Wild

+*+× ^·∨·^

NATURE

THank You--- Spirits---

Yes…. YES!!!   A heart-made
hand-written
Poem might

even….

Be…. A………

Prayer

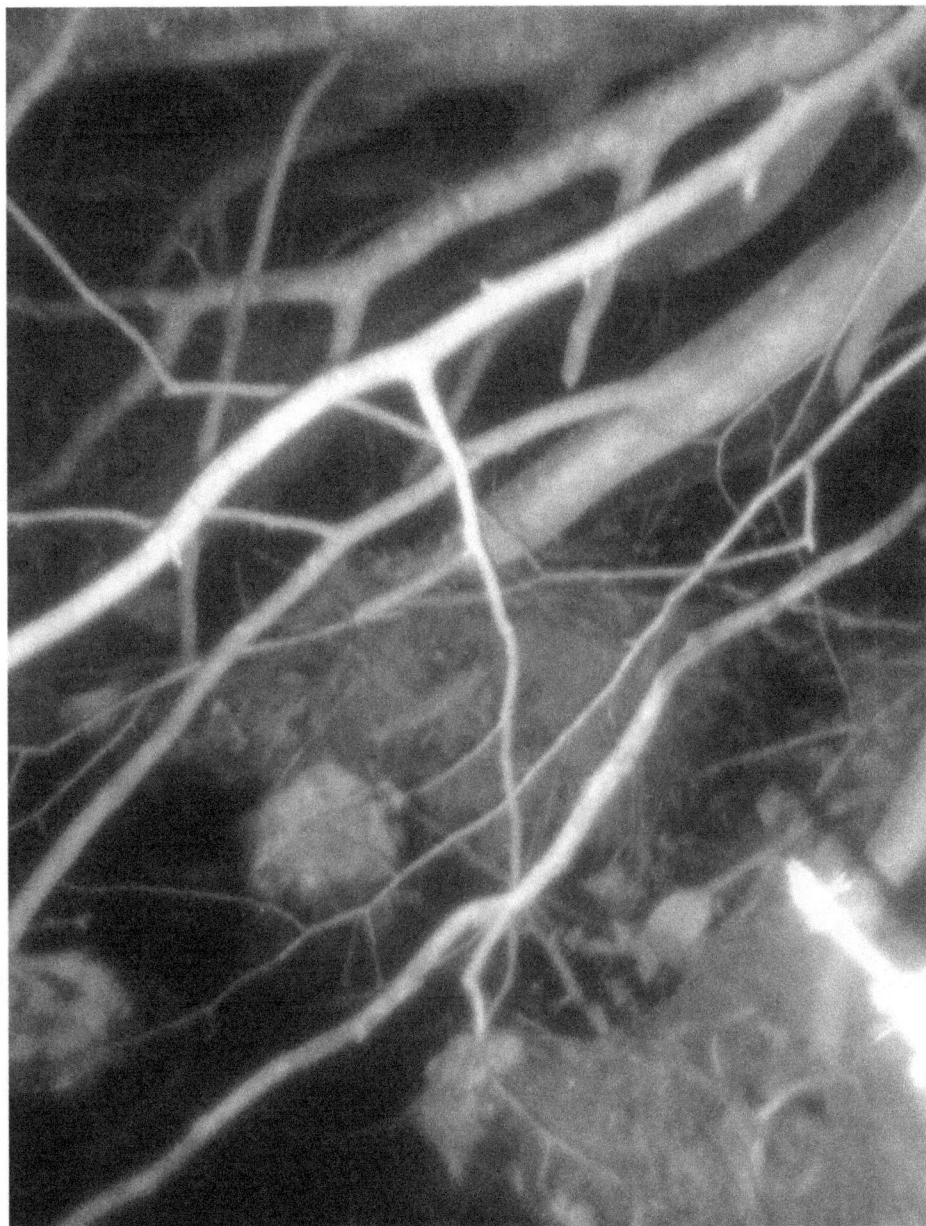

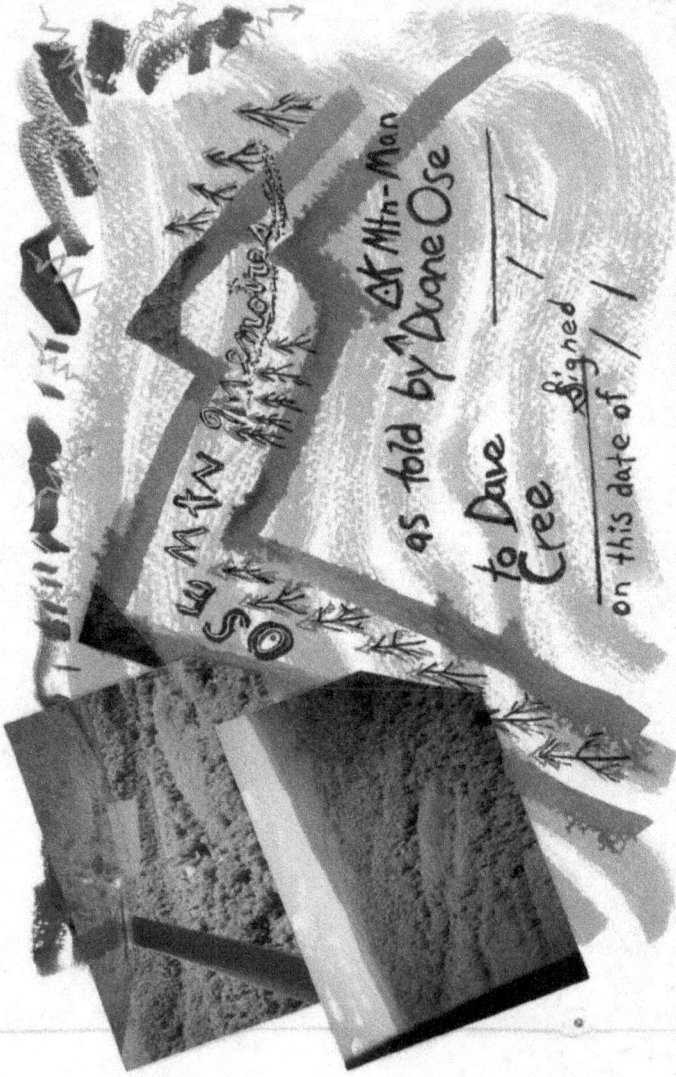

Sir Man Memoires

of K Mtn-Man

as told by Diane Ose

to Dave Cree

signed

on this date of / /

... from the Minnesota farm boy thrilling to Grandfather's old stories.... To a high production building
contractor in the Twin Cities area.... Quite a personal journey.... But…. Nowhere
near

our

Story's end….

(Graphic Arts…. Thanks to our mutual friend, Melanie

Many dream

..but few achieve their dreams
and by doing so,
inspire others.

OSE MOUNTAIN

Dunhill…. United Kingdom)

Now…. Let me introduce you to
Alaskan Mtn-Man Duane Arthur
Ose…. And me….

Good Old Duane….

Not only was Co-Author Ose last to
stake and file a claim under the 1862

Federal Homesteading Act.... But....
In a world of 2 week limits on a
recreational campsite.... Sat
phones.... AND far far less
SURVIVAL Know-How....

Yes.... Duane may very well prove
out to be "Last of THe Alaskan Mtn-
Men"

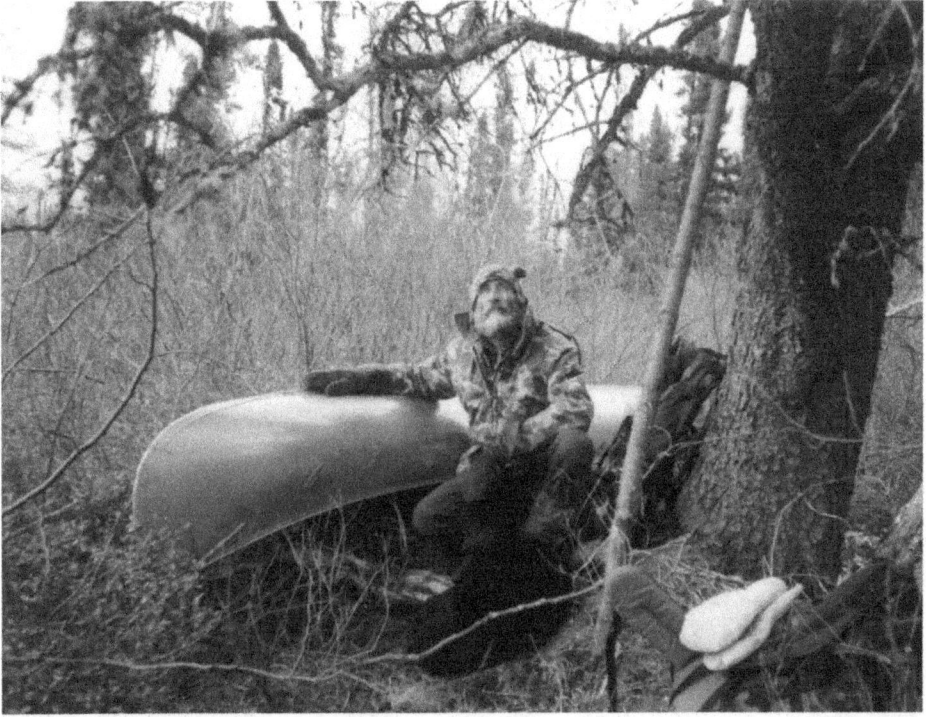

You know me.... Dave Cree.... My
Wild PlAces.... Better for me than
their silver n' gold.... YeA- MAybe
even better than their
                heaven....

+*++ ^.V.^ ++*+....

Now....
        Let The Real
                Action....

        Begin....

… swapping SURVIVAL Stories with my fellow Mountain-Man and Memoires Co-Author, Duane Ose….

+⚠+⚠*+ *808* +*⚠+⚠+

… THere was that Big Moon night out on THe Broadback….
It was nearing the end of October…. In quiet little coves and open
moonlit bays…. All along boulder-strewn riverbank and

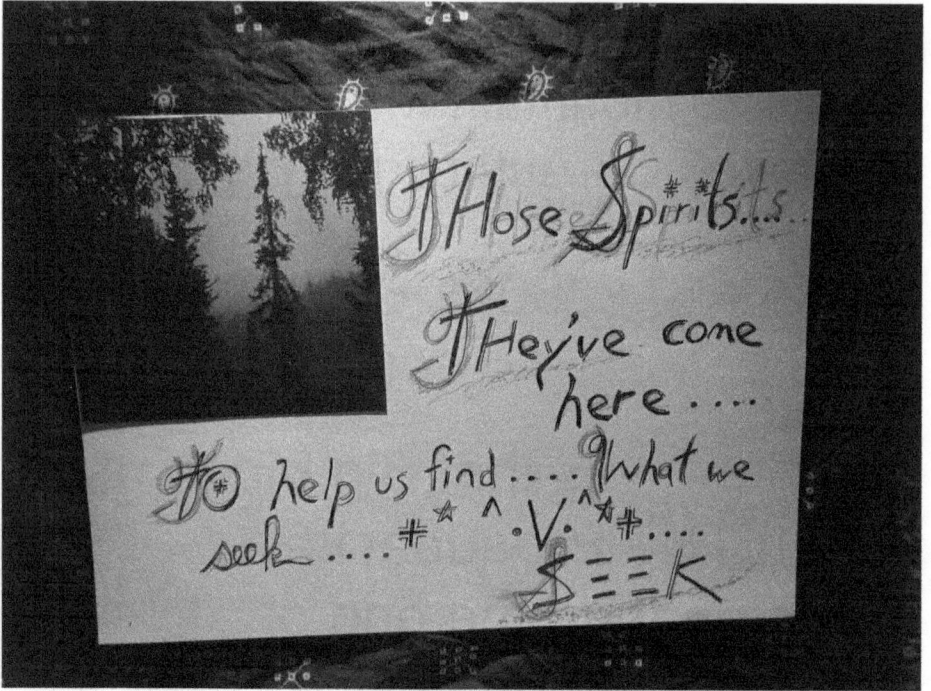

#Hose Spirits...
#Hey've come here ....
 # help us find .... What we
*seek ....# * ^.V.^*# ....*
$ ≡≡ K

sand beaches…. Ice was forming

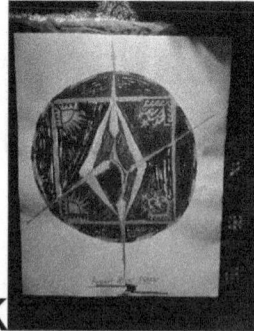

on THe Broadback

+*^.V.^*+

SURVIVAL

("Moon Over River-Ice".... Cree Artist Cynthia Saganash; Cree Nation of Waswanipi, QC Canada)

This was happening all along water's edge.... A lone paddler hoping for one last outing before Freeze-Up was pushing his luck.... A little too far

Many an October morning had seen a delicate skim of ice along water's edge.... By midmorning.... The night's ice had vanished.... But now--- Tonight--- There was a serious difference--- THe Broadback was freezing up in earnest

...+...&... THe same Finality.... Grim and inescapable.... THe Finality of vanes of new-formed ice shooting out across the River.... Locking the Broadback in their wintry grip

THat Grim Finality.... And inescapably--- Instinctively--- He knows that things are very very rapidly going from bad to.... Worse

...+.... &

...+.... &.... At first the Canoe's own weight was sufficient to break her way shoreward.... He drove her bow ahead with fervent strokes of the paddle.... Forcing the bow atop the ice sheet

But the time soon came when bow's weight alone was not enough....

Climbing further up on the thickening ice his craft was becoming

unstable.... Dangerously.... Unstable

Had he paddled too far out before turning shoreward? Would the Freeze-Up trap him on the River? Could he reach the shore by backing his canoe and chopping with his paddle? Now that there was no unfrozen water left to paddle in????

Would his energy last? Would his desperate measures be enough? Or would he die trying? Heart Attack! Midriver?

Unanswered questions.... Arms that screamed for relief.... For a rest.... Was it an inner voice .... Or a Guardian Spirit.... THat commanded--- "Don't Stop Now!"...."Get In Off THat River!!!"

THe Big October Moon had blurred overhead in the night sky.... THe River and the canoe and the Freeze-Up had all become a swaying bobbing nightmare.... How long had it taken him to break his way back to shore? And stumble his way back to camp???

Only THe River knows....

⚠

SURVIVAL.... Skills.... And Arts....
AND *Magic*....

+⚠+⚠*+ *808* +*⚠+⚠+

An Ose Mountain THinker….. He's connecting now…. With his Ose Ancestors….

My Co-Author's approach to SURVIVAL is entirely different from my own…. Duane Arthur Ose is a frontiersman of the old flintlock tradition--- "lock, stock…. N' octagonal barrel"…. No LOL

His nonfiction prose…. Like his life…. Is Frontier-Style--- To THe Bone

He tells his Survival Story straight from the hip…. Not a shred of academic pretensions here---

Co-Author Ose's first book--- <u>Alaskan</u> <u>Wilderness</u> <u>Adventure: Book 1</u>--- is an Adventure Story…. And more…. A seasoned outdoorsman, the author leaves his readers with no doubts as to his Alaska-Size grasp of his subject matter…. In his detailed account of his first trip into the Upper Kantishna wilderness of the Alaskan interior--- Ose tells of how he and his 15 year old Son, Dan, backpacked 50+ miles into an area recently opened for homesteading….

DUANE ARTHUR OSE

ALASKAN *wilderness*
ADVENTURE I

JOIN DUANE AND HIS SON DANIEL
ON A JOURNEY DEEP IN THE ALASKAN
WILDERNESS IN SEARCH OF FINDING
A NEW HOME

Duane writes--- "Book 1.... Says it all on how to survive. High ground; know how to treat and prevent drinking bad water; good fertile soil; firm ground; big timber; capturing and storing water....

Keep the body temp warm.... Disinfect all wounds.... Walk slow and deliberately.... Garden not on flat ground but on drainage ground (sloping ground.... Good gradient)

Build house on lee side of hill facing the sun.... Build the house where over-looking a view for miles and miles....To prevent feeling closed in.... Stack firewood more then 60ft from house....

Measure 3 times.... Cut once ....

When hiking.... Collect rain water to drink by using poly sheeting.... Carry signal flares.... Carry a first aid kit and antibiotics.... Carry a bear gun.... Bolt action.... 30/06/180gr .... Or 12 Ga Mag/Rifled Slugs.... Back packers food.... Tent.... Matches....Rain gear....

Prepare your SURVIVAL List.... By going from room to room in your house to remind you of what you might need....Kitchen ... Food.... Cooking utensils etc.... Bathroom....Bedroom... Etc... Etc....

Again….. Ose Mountain was planned…. Nothing was left to chance"

"Be prepared for every thing. Plan…. Plan…. PLAN…."

"And when a Woman's Voice whispers in your ear saying--- "

Choose Me"…. That's when you know….

that you're on the right place to live & die happy…."

"Yup…. That's just exactly how it happened…. How I was informed of THe Exact Right Spot to stake and claim…. Under federal Homestead Act…. Where to excavate…. Where to build…."

Ose Mountain Memoires – Book 1

DUGOUT

Dug into their Mountainside

An Alaskan
Home-Sweet-Home

Duane's new
float plane
base....Levi
Lake

log house....
Under
construction

"As a former scout master…. To be prepared Is the Boy Scout moto*

"Life is an Adventure"

"Shot my first Deer at age 9....

Pretender I am not.... I am a doer"

+*+* + *+*+

At the very deepest root of our Spirituality.... THere's a SURVIVAL Story.... Even though it's particulars.... It's fine details.... Are veiled in mists of prehistoric times--- Insights....

Emerge....

From out of the Grey

.... mist

A SURVIVAL Story.... A SURVIVAL Tradition.... A SURVIVAL Legacy.... It was in Do-

Or-Die situations.... That our primeaval predecessors uttered their first prayer.... First reached out.... TO Powers....

Beyond....

THank You--- First Nations....

+*+×

^·V·^....

(Cree Artist, Cynthia Saganash, Cree Nation of Waswanipi, QC, Canada)

In hopes of deepening our Readers' grasp of Book 2's SURVIVAL theme.... I highly recommend a classic Canadian documentary--- "Cree Hunters of Mistissini"

This incredible film.... An horizon-broadening view into the reality that SURVIVAL in remote Northern Latitudes is an absolutely consuming part of daily existence.... 24/7

Here we go....

    Weaving in....
      Cree Hunters.... Nomads of THe Pleistocene.... Afoot on the snow-drifted river ice.... Under Hunger Moons....

Guardian Spirits whisper--- "Lessons of Snow-TRail Creek.... "

... O--- Northlands.... What an amazing wealth of SURVIVAL Knowledge you and your First Nations Peoples have acquired.... To be able to live in such savage latitudes....

Always blows my mind.... To think of Ancestors....

Cree Anskiushuuch.... Inuit Hunters.... Living

without stoves....

Without steel axes and saws.... Without modern hunting equipment

(Painting.... Cree Artist, Cynthia Saganash, Cree Nation of Waswanipi, QC, Canada)

And surviving in their Subarctic and Arctic homelands for countless millennia before the whiteman's arrival in North America

... +.... &.... O! O! O!

O!!!   Northlands!!!

A Cree Hunter.... Of the Pleistocene.... His brave little band.... Beneath Hunger Moons.... They've been out

THere.... Afoot on the wind-swept river-ice.... For ever.... Ever so long...........

Starvation.... Grim and spectral.... It's punished them.... Pushed them.... And pushed them.... Closer....

And ever closer....

To THe Raw Edge....
Of themselves

Tonight.... Underneath yet another of the Midwinter's brutal Hunger Moons.... They make their brave little Camp just into the edge of the river timber.... In where there's a windbreak of riverbank Black Spruce protecting them from the wintry savagery of the river wind

He drums.... He dreams.... He's needing to see beyond the ordinary scene.... He's reaching.... Out/to/Powers/beyond....

And somehow.... In some mysterious and magical way.... He's found THe Hope that they needed to find.... In order to survive

+*+× ^·V·^.... Gives ya the shivers....

Doesn't it....

×+*+

We drum.... We dream.... Reaching out/to/Powers/beyond.... And it's as if a mysterious and magical/Key hath.... Once again been turned....

In a mysterious and

magical(ﾉ °□°) ﾉ ⌒ ┻━┻

LOCK....

A mysterious and magical/Door swings/wide.... (ﾉ °□°) ﾉ ⌒ ┻━┻

And here we've found THe Hope.... Inside.... THat we need to

+*+× ^·V·^

SURVIVE

Have come to believe that the response we get.... In reaching out to Powers Beyond.... Is directly proportional to THe Degree of our Need

It's being in EXTREME NEED.... That's what turns THe Magical Key.... In Mysticism's Magical Lock

Yea--- THe Seeker in Extreme Need is an extremely motivated Seeker indeed

Yes! Yes! YES!!!! If Necessity is THe Mother of Invention.... THen TRagedy is THe Father off our Collective Spirituality

... +.... &.... A Cree Hunter.... Of the Pleistocene.... They've been afoot.... Out THere.... On the wind-swept river-ice for ever so long.... AND now.... THey are here with us.... *In Spirit*

Tonight.... Underneath another Hunger Moon.... We make our own brave little Camps.... Just into the edge of the river timber.... In where there's a windbreak of riverbank Black Spruce protecting us from the savagery of the river wind.... And our Ancestors.... THey're here with us.... *In Spirit*

In Spirit.... We drum.... We dream.... We reach out/to/Powers/beyond....

And somehow.... In some mysterious and magical way.... We too have found THe Hope that we needed to find.... In order to survive....

+*+× ^·V·^.... ×+*+

Comes a SURVIVAL Experience of my own.... Relying upon a Medicine-Song.... "Good-Medicine.... Good-Spirits.... Brother Oswegatchie...."...."O! Medicine--- Be Strong".... Guardian Spirits whisper--- "Lessons of Snow-TRail Creek"

Ahh.... Questing.... Exploring.... Yes.... Venturing out into uncharted depths.... Our SURVIVAL Stories....

O! Ever so complexly interwoven with our Spirituality.... Our Beliefs

In the spirit of "Cree Hunters of Mistissini".... Co-Author Ose and I hope to cut through all of the preconceptions and romanticized illusions.... To share a knowledge of SURVIVAL that will encourage our readers to venture out into Wilderness on their own.... And do so without undue risk.... Surviving to tell SURVIVAL Stories of their own

…+…. &…. Mtn-Man Ose tells of an Ose Mountain Winter Solstice

"… the two Mountains…. On skyline…. Denali…. To the left….
Mount Four-Acre is on the right…. V notch in the mountaintop is
where the name "Four-Acre" comes from

Denali Mountain is exactly 77 miles true South…. Not magnetic—
but true South of my window

On the shortest day of the year…. December 22nd…. Winter
Solstice Day…That precious golden Sun is behind the peak of the
Mountain…. We get 3 hours of Sun….
By holding an arm up and spreading little finger and big finger
apart…. That's the travel distance of the Sun…. 3 hours of sunshine

Shortest day of the year

+*+*+*….. Hi Dave….. First thing to make clear…. At noon precisely
the shortest day….. The sun is just behind the peak shining out…..
You see the Golden Disc…. Light of the Sun…. That's high noon and
the very next day at noon the sun is on top of Denali mountain

The spacing I use is I hold out my arm at full length in front of me
directed towards Denali mountain pulling the thumb outward and the
little finger outward between the point of the sum and the point of the
little finger is the time travel of 3 hours and you point your fist at
Denali mountain…. Sun rises in the East…. Sets in the West…. 3
hours later

Again hold one arm in front of you with the three fingers folded down
into the palm and extending your little finger to the right and your left
and your thumb to the left

Again close your fist point your little finger to the West point your
thumb to the east directed at the Denali mountain and on the
shortest day of the year the sun setting behind the peak you still see
the rays of light like on a dollar bill behind the symbol…. Between
your thumb and the little finger is the time of travel of 3 hours…. We

are precisely 100 miles south of the Arctic circle the Arctic circle is where you have zero light on the shortest day

O! Readers…. Can't you just taste how utterly essential it was to an Alaskan Mtn-Man's SURVIVAL…. To center himself in that wonderful Winter Solstice Day Sunlight

Duane continues--- "I know this may seem complicated but it was important to me while I was there…. The giant sundial Denali Mountain…. I was fortunate enough to pick a location where this measuring device was visible…. Right there on my skyline

As to the name "Four Acre"…. I think you can find that out by googling it I do not remember what I was told about it all these mountains are in the Alaskan mountain chain what we call the Alaska range

Some 300 miles south of me south of Ose Mountain is Anchorage…. We used to get three TV channels from Anchorage before they changed to digital…. Denali Mountain was a natural formation that bounced the signal down to us. All this time we had a multi-channel huge TV antenna that we could watch TV…. Even in our Dugout…. But when they changed from analog to digital we lost the signal

So the unique thing about Ose Mountain…. In our house site…. Is that we are precisely located to utilize Denali mountain as our sundial

The first holiday in history was a pagan holiday the 25th of December…. Rejoicing that the Sun returneth…. It was gradual at first and by the 25th they were convinced…. The sun is returning

25th of December…. Now Christmas…. But in the beginning it was a pagan holiday…. Jesus Christ I believe was born in April…. But they rearranged it to be the 25th of December

Somewhat like Indian name for Denali Mountain…. "Big Bear" or "THe Great One" and then Denali Mountain…. And then assassinated President McKinley…. Put his name on the mountain and now the mountain is back to this rightful owner Denali…. No man should put his name on a natural monument that was another name first

I believe I have the right to call our Mountain Ose Mountain because I was the first…. It is not a lodge…. It is a private home."

+*++* +8+ *++*+

"Everybody….

Out !"

Whew…. THat's SURVIVAL….
Mtn-

Woman Style

O!

SURVIVAL….

Alaska-Style!

*+*THX\ 808 /XHT*+*

… it was deep of Winter…. A "Big Snows"* Winter…. 5 feet of snow blanketed the land…. Six miles of unbroken trail lay ahead…. Six miles--- And what grueling miles they were---

*"Honor of the Big Snows", a novel by James Oliver Curwood

"I'd snowshoed to the neighbor's place.... In preparations for bringing home a recently purchased snowmobile.... And there was only one way to get it home.... 6 miles of trail had to be packed down solid enough to support snowmachine and operator"

"I had to take half steps--- Not just walking my trail--- but widening it as well to keep the snowmachine from slipping off the side of what I'd packed down with my snowshoes....

I'd slide the snowshoe forward--- Press down--- Stand in place to bring my full weight to bear--- And then repeat the sliding step with the other shoe.... Slide.... Press down.... Stand.... Half steps.... Shake the snow off the snowshoe.... Keep on putting one snowshoe ahead of the other.... The hours going by"

Those hours went by so much faster than the miles.... 5 feet of snow.... 6 miles over.... And another 6 miles back.... And all at an agonizingly slow pace as required for packing down his trail "Somebody must have been praying for an Alaskan Mtn-Man.... By the name of Duane Arthur Ose.... THat night

...+...&.... In his account of preparing a snowshoe trail for the purpose of bringing home a snowmachine from a neighbor's 6 mile distant homestead--- My Co-Author leaves the reader with no doubts as to what a wealth of experience and savvy Mountain Man Ose's hand-to-hand Survival Style brings to how he meets the challenges--- the obstacles--- that life in his Alaskan Wilds regularly puts squarely in his path

As he and Wife Rena.... Worked their

way….

From their 9x11 Mtnside
Dugout,,,,,

An Alaskan Home
Sweet Home

"Dugout"….
Book 1 Ose Mtn
Memoires

To
Log House....

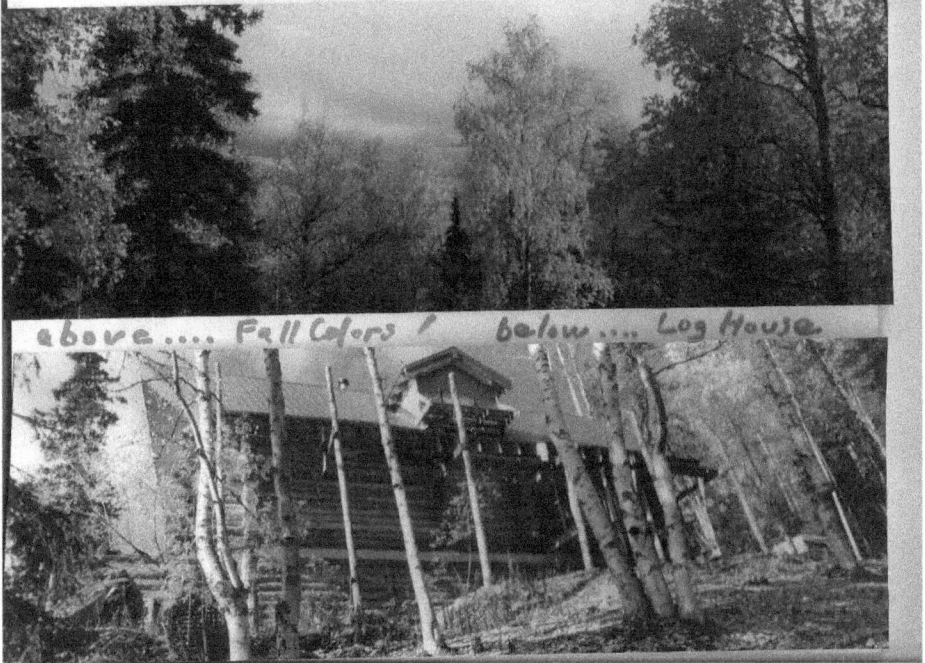

above.... Fall Colors / below.... Log House

DBL00/IMPACT

SURVIVAL

(Photographer Brendan Forward, Cree Nation of Mistissini, Quebec, Canada)

SURVIVAL....
Alaska-
Style

As Co-Author Ose and I have worked our way through this project--- SURVIVAL has emerged as an utterly 24/7 theme.... Our shared experiences in meeting and grappling with the challenges of life in wilderness convince us that we each have our own personal approach to Survival.... Our own instinctive style

Duane Arthur Ose's Memoires fill the pages of an Alaska-Size Memory-Journal.... Ahhh--- We take a step back and try to take in the sweep of it all.... We rub our eyes.... We're overwhelmed by Wilderness.... Overwhelmed by the epic sweep of life in the remote interior wilds of Alaska

No wonder that Alaskans have long honored their homeland as the "Land of THe Last Frontier"

Ahhh.... Ose Mountain Story in Mountain-Man Ose's own words--- His own distinctively "frontier" writing style.... Duane and I are always reminding eachother that we don't want the story of frontier life to sound like something written by an academic--- far from the frontier world of hardships and survival challenges that leave little time for perfecting one's literary technique…. Yes--- Co-Author Ose's voice as a writer is a voice full of strong identity and high self-esteem…. It's a strong voice because it's founded on the personal bed-rock of being an Alaskan…. Having staked his claim to an upper Kantishna homesite just as the Federal Homestead Act ceased to be--- Duane's Ose Mountain Story spans the bredth of 2 chapters in the state's history…. As homesteading under the 1862 Act came to a close, an Old Alaska drew herself deeper back into the mists and myths of the past And a new chapter in the Alaska Story began…. From 1990 to 2019, Duane and his late wife, Rena, lived the wilderness life--- Earning themselves and their beloved Ose Mountain a well-deserved place in the bigger story of Alaska

Alaska-Size? As the details of the Ose's 30 plus years residency on Ose Mountain come into view--- We're convinced that Alaska-Size is no exaggeration

…+… &… am thinking back now on my Co-Author's account of breaking trail through 5 feet of snow…. His "half-steps"…. 6 miles worth of "half-steps"…. Yes--- There are times when a SURVIVAL challenge becomes nothing short of an ordeal…. Returning to his Dugout home…. That Winter night deep in the Alaskan Wilds…. A SURVIVAL Ordeal if ever there was one!!

Duane continues his account--- "… 2nd thoughts were going through

my mind…. Had my plan to break trail the full 6 miles--- In one night-

-- Been overly ambitious? Would it not be better to break my Trail-

Breaking Project up into 2 or 3 day's work?? Something inside me

kept putting one snowshoe ahead of the other…. One

Snowshoe……… Ahead of THe

Other…"

"I was working myself into A SURVIVAL TRance"

"The final rise of the land.... A final uphill section of trail.... By now my sweat-soaked clothing was a frozen suit of armor.... The frozen clothing not only hampered my trail-breaking efforts.... But threatened my body warmth.... Threatened my body's biological ability to stave off hypothermia.... And Survive..."

"... that final rise.... An Ordeal.... A SURVIVAL nightmare.... But now was no time for changing the Plan.... It was one of those times when an Ordeal brings out our SURVIVAL Instinct in its purest and most unstoppable form.... I knew that I had to make it home.... If I didn't make it home.... Plain and simple... I was going to die out there.... Alone"

...+...&... "... A Golden-Yellow Rectangle of Light--- There In the darkness of an Alaskan mountainside

"... that Golden-Yellow Rectangle was no figment of the imagination--- No Mystical Vision--- It was the plexiglass window in the door of the Dugout.... I'd survived--- I'd made it Home"

...+...&... And A Trance.... Had worked A Miracle

"... O--- Golden--- O--- Yellow and Bright and THe Promise of Warmth.... And then--- What had been A Golden-Yellow Rectangle--- Swung wide and opened--- And THere She was....

My Guardian Angel, Rena, was standing there in the Dugout's open doorway..."

... And A TRance--- Had worked it's
SURVIVAL ....

*+*THX\ MAGIC /XHT*+*

"... she must have heard me coming in from the trail.... Heard the tinkling and creaking of my ice-covered clothing.... Long as I live--- I'll never forget her first words--- Her Greeting--- "Get In Here""

"... My Rena..... She shoves into my hands a big full hot cup of cocoa and starts to undress me.... First the snowshoes,... Then the rest. She warmed me with her body hugging me. We were so happy. I'd shuffled in like a monster--- Snowshoes and all. The ICE MAN"

Hear that reminiscent/kinda dreamy tone come into Old Mtn-Man Ose's voice---

"... Rena.... Our Leader

Rena.... My Queen"

...+... ⚠....

Yes--- When it's Do-Or-Die--- Those Ose Mtn Oses do their surviving--- Side by side... Eye to eye....

THe Ose Mtn Story.... Yes! Here's An Alaska-Size

SURVIVAL

Story

++...&...& .+.+.+. &...&...+*+*

In an adoring husband's words....
"they broke the mold when they

made my Rena"

... +.... &....

⚠....

⚠....

Lookout.... Readers....

Now.... Here comes the dry....
Philosophize'n part.... Mtn-Man LOL!
[Photo of Duane in Cowboy hat]

This Matter of SURVIVAL.... More here than first meets the eye.... In thinking on this subject in the more fully thought out way that it's taking to write this Book.... THe Complexity of "SURVIVAL" is convincing me that a How-To Guide.... A Manual.... Is far beyond the scope of this Book

To take a comprehensive look at such a complex subject as Woodcraft.... A booklength subject in itself.... And then there's the matter of the many SURVIVAL Lessons.... Which can only be learned by years and years of personal experience.... Such lessons can be shared with our Readers.... But that's just barely the start of learning the Lesson for yourself.... And incorporating it into your own personal set of SURVIVAL Skills

Duane and I do plan to write our own Ose&Cree SURVIVAL Manual... But under a separate title

In the process of writing Ose Mtn Memoires.... Twin-Brother Don and I have often "agreed to disagree".... Case in point.... This well-known Jack London quote from his Wilderness Classic--- <u>The Call of the Wild</u>---

"... 2 or 3 fools.... More or less.... Will make no difference in the course of the world...."

London's 2 main characters have just met.... On a snowy bluff above the yet somewhat frozen Yukon River....

The complete novels of
White Fang, The Sea-Wolf,
The Call of the Wild and
Cruise of the Dazzler
plus 15 short stories...
with original illustrations

JACK LONDON
Tales of the North

"… 2 or 3 fools…. More or less…. Will make no difference in the course of the world…."

Am hereby strongly recommending that any and all Mtn-Men…. And/or Mtn-Women-in-Training…. Amongst our Readers…. Make this very special quote their very
own

Don't just commit it to memory…. Internalize it…. Make it part of your instinctive will to survive….

Let it's IMPACT sink in and manifest itself in THe Rockhard Set of yer jaw…. In THe Steely Glint in yer eyes….

… +…. &…. THe Message here…. Don't allow your lack of

experience to get you into life-threatening situations ….
Always…. Always…. ALWAYS---
"Better Safe Than Sorry"

⚠….

⚠….

Lest you come to be numbered in the company of London's "… 2 or 3 fools…."

Ose Mountain Memoires – Book 1

DUGOUT

Dug into their Mountainside

An Alaskan
Home-Sweet-Home

When out on the trail…. There are often nights when the shelter of an abandoned cabin…. Or mountain-side dugout…. is far beyond our prospects

On one such Night Duane's accommodations proved more comfortable than first expected…. His resourcefulness discovered a Dugout where most hikers would have only seen a barren shelterless mountaintop….

Gathering himself an ample supply of moss and lichen…. Digging himself a shallow "dugout" into the stony surface…. Lining his makeshift Dugout head to foot with a mossy padding…. He climbs in

Putting his feet down into his backpack…. Reaching out…. Duane pulls his blanket of mountaintop moss and lichens in on top of himself…. Morning finds the peak covered with glittering frost…. After a warm and dry night's rest…. An Alaskan Mtn-Man's readied himself for an early start

SURVIVAL.... A shallow trench dug into a mtntop....
Tents.... Dugouts.... Teepees.... His resourcefulness
kicks in and decides on a double-walled teepee...

Serving his need for shelter against the fierce cold of
an Alaskan Winter....

Double walls of canvas.... Packed with Meadow
Grasses for insulation.... "Just like the Plains
Indians"

Old Mtn-Man Ose.... No end to the variations on his
Alaskan SURVIVAL themes.... Can't resist a bit of
Mtn-Man LOL here.... Teepees.... And that
observation Duane shared with me.... Noticing me
flirting with the Cree ladies of Eeyou-Istchee.... On
Facebook

In his exact words--- "Not many women are gonna
go fer yer tents, Dave Cree...."

.... Hard guy to argue with....

What could I say?

By Gar--- THat's Alaskan Mtn-Man

Duane Arther Ose

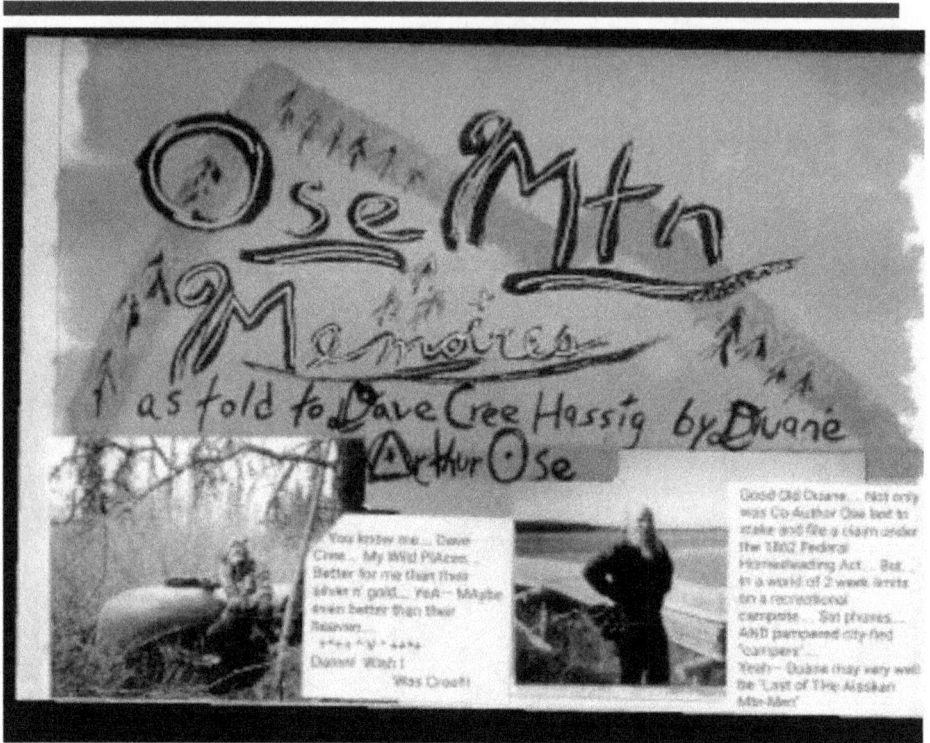

Ose Mtn Memoires

as told to Dave Cree Hassig by Duane Arthur Ose

That darn Duane….

Being kinda slow on figuring out how to reply to something as kinda "Hmmmm" as this…. Facebook comes to mind…. I'll show him…. Lol…. Mtn-Man LOL…. Mtn-Man who laughs last…. Laughs…. Best

Now…. Back to Mtn-Man SURVIVAL…. Duane's trail-breaking experience…. An Alaskan Big Snows Winter…. 5 feet of it on the level…. 6 miles over to the neighbor's cabin for the newly purchased snowmachine….

SURVIVAL…. Alaska-
        Style….

Arriving at the isolated cabin…. Having just broken trail through 5 feet of snow…. O! THose 6 gruelingly herculean miles….

How tired you must have been…. But without even taking your snowshoes off…. You're on to your next SURVIVAL Challenge…. SURVIVAL Question of the moment…. How to spend the night here…. In a cabin…. Little more than an uninsulated shack??

Ah-Ha! With an Action Plan leaping instinctively to mind…. Mtn-Man Ose sets to work….

We've all noticed how the wind-swirled snow will drift around a tree trunk…. A boulder…. Leaving an open place between snowdrift and boulder…. Such the snow…. Drifted high as the eaves…. Drifted 'round this little cabin's walls….

SURVIVAL Instinct taking hold…. He commences to shoulder the eave-high drifts in against the cabin walls…. 'Round the cabin he goes….

An uninsulated and drafty cabin will now be a seriously more comfortable place to spend a long Alaskan Winter's night…. He prepares fire-building kindling in the little wodstove and lights the fire….

Yep…. THat's vintage Mtn-Man SURVIVAL….

SURVIVAL…. Alaska-Style

WHY IS SHE CRYING?

Canadian author Grey Owl.... An immigrant to the Americas.... His eye witness account of the slaughter of the Buffalo on the Great Plains is one of the most impassioned and deeply thought out commentaries that I have read on the subject.... The Buffalo in their 10s of millions reduced to a single herd.... Corraled in Texas.... Ahh--- From

10s of millions to a ghostly remnant.... In barely 2 decades

Grey Owl's account of these events goes beyond an historic record of events.... Leaving no doubt in his readers' minds as to how strongly he disapproved of an ecological atrocity of such horrible magnitude

Grey Owl.... Author.... Historian.... Visionary....
. And an early voice on the side of respecting THe Land and consuming Natural Resources in an Earth-Friendly and responsible manner.... With moderation

What would he think of the fires that are still burning across Eeyou-Istchee.... Given the fact that these wildfires are larger and burning hotter.... More destructively.... As a result of the extensive clearcutting practiced in the Province of Quebec?

Selected from Author Grey Owl's <u>The Men of the Last Frontier</u>.... "THe TRail"

... reading from pages 78-79.... From a Book to be read and reread....

"Stars paling in the East.... Breath that whistles through the nostrils.... And hangs in the frosty air like steam

Tug of the tump line.... Swing of the snowshoes....
Sets of tracks made in the snow.... Every one.... A
story

Hissing.... Slanting sheets of snow.... Swift rattle of
snowshoes over an unseen trail in the dark

A groundcloth of canvas.... A long fire.... And a roof
of smoke.... Silence

Canoes gliding between palisades of rock....
Teepees.... Smoke-dyed.... Out there on a smooth
point.... In amongst the Red Pines.... Inscrutable
faces peering out

Little fires by darkling streams.... Slow wind of
evening hovering in the tree tops.... Passing on to
nowhere

Gay caparisoned clouds moving in review... Under a
setting sun.... Fading day.... Pictures forming.... And
fading away.... In glowing embers

Voices in the running waters.... Calling.... Calling....
The Lone cry of a Loon from an unseen Lake....
Peace.... Contentment.... THis is THe Trail"

Good old Grey Owl…. His frontier-style poetry…. Who could read his pages without deeply sensing the frontiersman's profound connectedness to THe Land…. My Heart is pained by a growing gulf between the Land-connectedness of the Last Frontiersmen…. And that of today

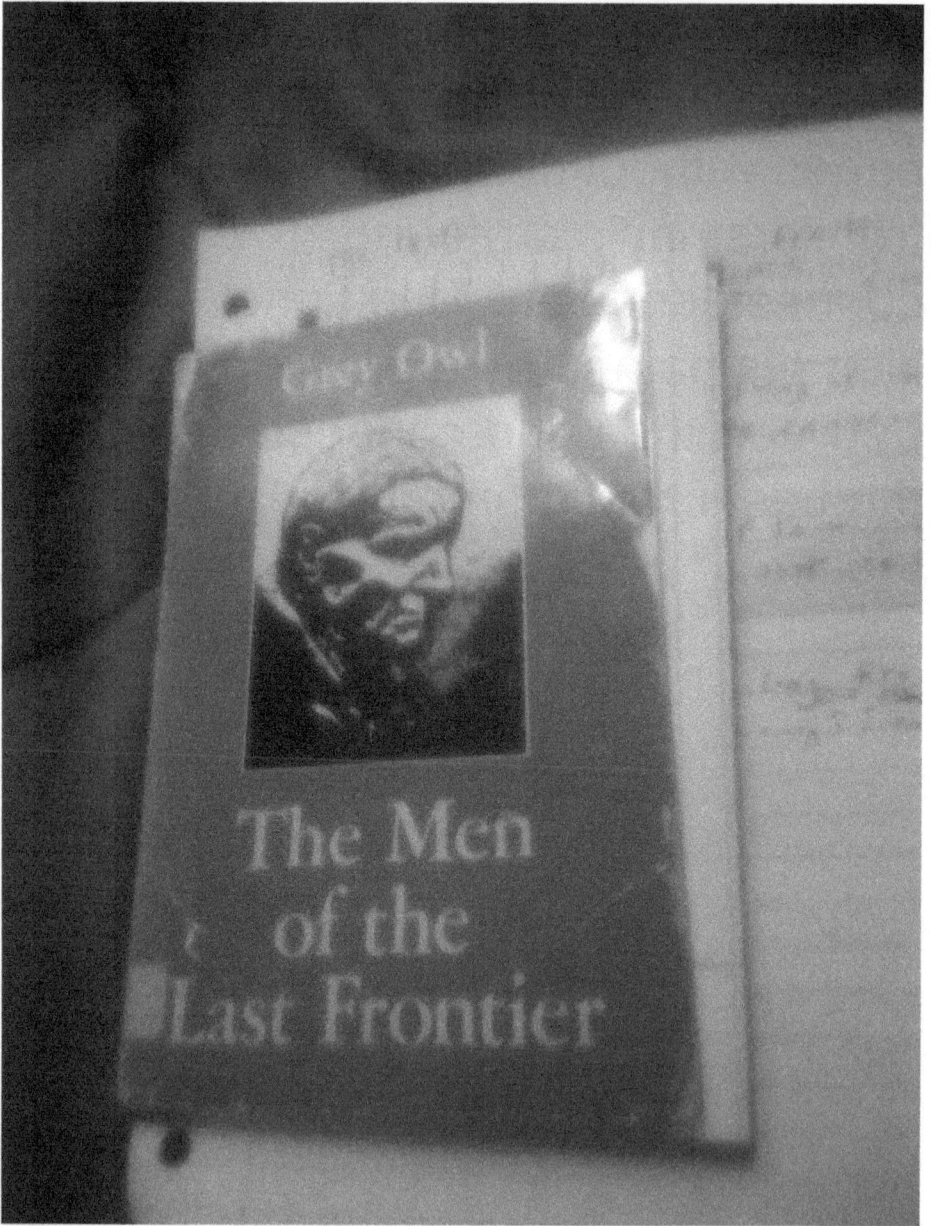

"Tear down the tent and the shelter…. Stars pale for the breaking of day…. Far over the hills lies Canada…. Let us be up…. And upon our way"….

TRail Song….

TH8…… ^•V•^…. ……8HT

Lights….

Go down…. And
THe Curtain….

TH8…… ^•V•^…. ……

8HT

FALLS

AND now….. For a real serious change of Scene…. THe Scene…. Goes expanding outward…. By leaps…. And bounds

Again….
    Our Earth-Mother….
    Why is She
        Crying?????

WHY IS SHE CRYING?

Ahhh…. This theme of SURVIVAL…. So very much more than first meets the eye….

SURVIVAL…. Of an individual…. Of a species…. Yes--- even of an entire ecosystem….

Planet Earth Herself!

AND then there's the question of whether our species will survive…. On a self-centered greed-driven rampage…. Or on an Earth-Friendly Path…. Will Homo sapiens continue to stumble along on our various paths of greed and materialistic self-centeredness…. The answer's unclear

SURVIVAL Questions…. Will we as heritors of the legacy of "thinking man" answer these questions in an Earth-Friendly and carefully thought out manner…. Or will we continue to fall short of our "thinking man" legacy???

I believe that future generations of those who have chosen to reside out there along the raw edge of "civilization"…. And beyond… Could play a key role in leading Homo sapiens feet upon Earth-Friendly Paths and Trails

O! Readers--- Let's all try to be broadminded as can be here…. Try expanding upon our theme of SURVIVAL With our own numbers now approaching the unthinkable 4 Billion mark…. Now's the time to extend our awareness of SURVIVAL out into Earth-Conscious Dimensions…. How 'bout making the shift from Alaska-Style…. To an Earth-Friendly Style? An Earth-Friendly Style of SURVIVAL adopted by everybody…. Everywhere…. Let THe Billions walk an Earth-Friendly Path….

Let THe Billions

Smile….

An Earth-Friendly

+*+× ^•V•^ SMILE

So many Good Questions…. But on a Planet where our numbers are now fast closing in on the 4 Billion mark…. Lotsa Good Questions we need to be asking ourselves…. Not just quietly asked in the relatively comfortable quiet of our own minds…. But….

Asking each other…. Our multiple layers of government…. Our
Collective Soul

O! SURVIVAL…. Quite an extremely complex and even thorny Subject we have here….

James Bay Railroad??

??*???? * ????*??

"James Bay Railroad"? No---
"Mining Company Railroad"….

$$$$$$$$$$$$$$$....

As our western world'$ appetite for an ever e$calating level of per capita con$umption of Natural Resource$.... Drive$ all $ector$ of the Natural Resource$ indu$trie$ to expand....
Expand....

EXPAND....

Sharing the following letter.... Recently submitted to newspapers here in NE US and Eastern Canada

James Bay Railroad/Letter to Editor

https://docs.google.com/document/d/1qu65ho20aSAUNub3i9YYMeTUFIDw6ENs/edit?usp=drivesdk&ouid=117008596031411852371&rtpof=true&sd=true

From: Dave Hassig <davehassig@gmail.com>
Date: Wed, May 3, 2023, 9:02 AM
Subject: JAMES BAY RAILROAD

To: Ottawa Outdoors, Editor, Dave Brown/Ottawa Citizen <editor@ottawaoutdoors.ca>

For the past 50 years, the James Bay Region of western Quebec has been the focus of a series of on-going Natural Resources "development" campaigns.... First road-building.... Then a series of hydro projects, which have been done in an extremely Earth-Unfriendly manner.... Huge reservoirs; diversion of entire rivers--- resultung in mercury poisoning of Fish and Wildlife.... And very likely--- poisoning of the James Bay's Cree inhabitants whose traditional way of life depends on food from their homeland's Fish and Wildlife resources

Uncontrolled clearcutting of millions of hectares of old growth Forest Lands.... Inadequately regulated mining projects.... Gold.... Lithium....

And now a new railroad.... Escalating the pace of development to what most of us would recognize as a Natural Resources Rampage

It's heart-breaking to see this happening.... Visiting for 40 years has brought these issues to be near and dear to my Heart

A new railroad.... Extending rail lines 100s of kilometers northward will result in a virtual explosion of new mines.... This when the existing mines and refineries have a dangerously Earth-Unfriendly environmental record.... Vast areas of unreclaimed tailings.... Uncontrolled air and water pollution

Please help us educate about this.... Natural Resources from the Canadian North are part of a global economy.... Products manufactured using minerals from Canadian mines.... And hydroelectricity generated in Quebec's vast hydro projects are being consumed right here in the NE US.... For Americans to turn a blind eye upon

Resource Rampages in the Canadian Northlands.... Nothing short of environmental racism... +....
&....

Why can't we agree that if things are left to the economic developers.... To the corporate executives.... To the hydro and sawmill and mining company CEOs— Wreck of THe Planet

If the future of our Earth is left up to those motivated solely by $$$$ profits— Wreck of THe Planet

Why can't we agree that the "American Dream"....
"Sea to shining sea".... Is an environmental
nightmare of global proportions— Wreck of The
Planet

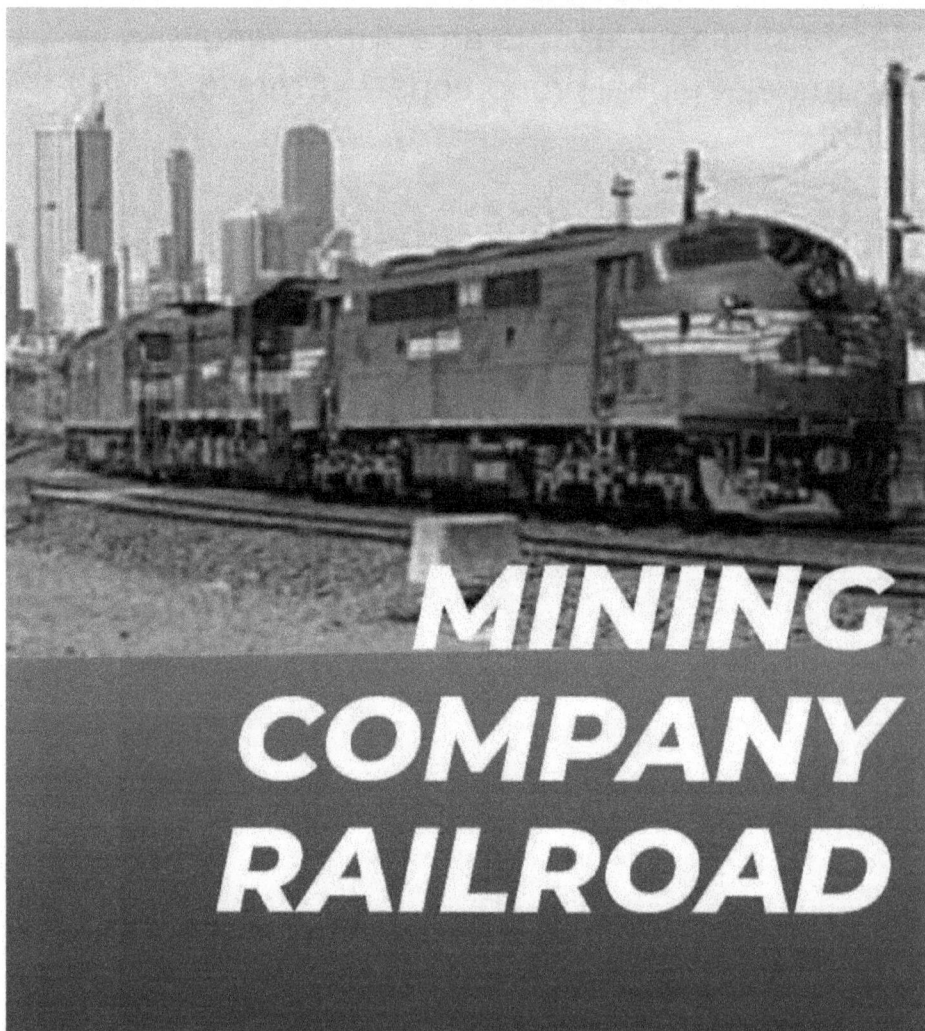

MINING COMPANY RAILROAD

Please— Homo sapiens—PLEASE! Take a step back from our species' long history of materialism.... A history tragically flawed by its lack of an Earth-Friendly awareness--- Let's all open-mindedly ask ourselves--- "Can our Earth's 3rd World Billions all live at the same per capita level of Natural Resources consumption.... As the US.... Canada.....

Western Europe.... ????

⚠ .... ⚠ ....

WRECK OF THe PLANET....

Plan is to use this letter.... As part of an educational display.... Libraries.... Community centers, etc....

O! Yesssss..... Goin global

here

....

SURVIVAL.... "Alaska-Style"....

And now.... How 'bout SURVIVAL.... In an ever more Earth-Friendly

Style

??

How Else To Save THe

Planet!

Clearly, our next generation of Mtn-Men…. And Mtn-Women…. Needs to be taking mighty strides towards….

An Earth-
Friendly Style of SURVIVAL

Ose Mountain Memoires – Book 2

SURVIVAL

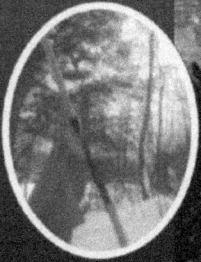

Alaska-Style

... THose
Spirits....

(Cree Photographer Wayne Rabbitskin, Cree Nation of Eeyou-Istchee, James Bay Canada)

Spirit-In-Everything
... above
... below
... and all about

THose Spirits…. THey've come here…. To help us find what we….

+*+× ^•V•^

SEEK

O! Planet Earth…. Spirit in

All

things

Yes…. TOwards an Earth-Friendly definition of Greater Good…. TOwards fulfillment of the promise of Homo "sapiens "

The answers to these SURVIVAL questions are up to us….

Happy and Earth-Friendly TRails to all of You…. From Good-Medicine Pond,
Late Spring, 2023

NOTES….

….

■ ■ ■

www.ingramcontent.com/pod-product-compliance
Lightning Source LLC
Chambersburg PA
CBHW032102020426
42335CB00011B/455